Totally AMAZING FACTS ABOUT DINOSAURS

MATHEW J. WEDEL

raintree

a Capstone company — publishers for children

COELOPHYSIS

TIME PERIOD LIVED: LATE TRIASSIC 235 TO 228 MILLION YEARS AGO

LOCATION: UNITED STATES AND SOUTH AFRICA

LENGTH: 3 METRES (9.8 FEET)

More than 1,000 **COELOPHYSIS** skeletons were found in a **SINGLE QUARRY** at Ghost Ranch, New Mexico, USA.

ONE OF THEM HAD THE BONES OF A SMALL CROCODILE INSIDE ITS RIBCAGE – ITS LAST MEAL!

EORAPTOR HAD **HOLLOW** BONES.

EORAPTOR

TIME PERIOD LIVED: LATE TRIASSIC 235 TO 228 MILLION YEARS AGO

LOCATION: ARGENTINA

LENGTH: 1 METRE (3.3 FEET)

Its hollow bones made it **LIGHTWEIGHT** and **SPEEDY.**

HERRERASAURUS

TIME PERIOD LIVED: LATE TRIASSIC
228 MILLION YEARS AGO

LOCATION: ARGENTINA

LENGTH: 3 METRES (9.8 FEET)

THIS DINOSAUR WALKED ON TWO LEGS AS IT HUNTED.

THREE TOES?

Herrerasaurus had five toes on each foot, but only three reached the ground!

LILIENSTERNUS WAS A FIERCE PREDATOR!

With its SHARP TEETH and CLAWS, it could easily ATTACK and bring down a young PLATEOSAURUS.

LILIENSTERNUS

TIME PERIOD LIVED: LATE TRIASSIC 235 TO 228 MILLION YEARS AGO

LOCATION: ARGENTINA

LENGTH: 3 METRES (9.8 FEET)

5

HORNS!

CARNOTAURUS

TIME PERIOD LIVED: LATE CRETACEOUS
84 TO 65 MILLION YEARS AGO

LOCATION: ARGENTINA

LENGTH: 7.6 METRES (25 FEET)

Carnotaurus is called "**MEAT BULL**" because of the horns over its eyes.

THIS SCALED PREDATOR WAS ONE OF THE FASTEST RUNNERS OF ITS TIME.

DAHALOKELY

TIME PERIOD LIVED: LATE CRETACEOUS
90 MILLION YEARS AGO

LOCATION: MADAGASCAR

LENGTH: 2.7 TO 4.3 METRES (9 TO 14 FEET)

Dahalokely means "SMALL THIEF" in Malagasy, the native language of Madagascar.

IT WASN'T VERY BIG – ONLY A BIT LARGER THAN A HUMAN.

7

MASIAKASAURUS

TIME PERIOD LIVED: LATE CRETACEOUS 72 TO 66 MILLION YEARS AGO

LOCATION: MADAGASCAR

LENGTH: 2 METRES (6.56 FEET)

MASIAKASAURUS HAD TEETH THAT POINTED FORWARDS.

ITS TEETH WERE ABLE TO GRAB SLIPPERY, SQUIRMY PREY SUCH AS FISH AND LIZARDS.

Like many **BUMP-HEADED** meat-eaters, Rugops had **WRINKLED BONES** on its skull.

RUGOPS

RUGOPS MEANS "ROUGH FACE".

TIME PERIOD LIVED: **MIDDLE CRETACEOUS 110 TO 93.5 MILLION YEARS AGO**

LOCATION: **NIGER**

LENGTH: **7 METRES (23 FEET)**

BARYONYX

TIME PERIOD LIVED: EARLY CRETACEOUS
130 MILLION YEARS AGO

LOCATION: UK AND SPAIN

LENGTH: 10 METRES (32 FEET)

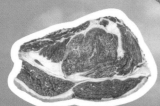

This dinosaur was a **SURF** and **TURF** eater! It liked **MEAT** and **SEAFOOD**.

ITS **JAWS** AND **TEETH** LOOKED MUCH LIKE THOSE OF TODAY'S CROCODILES.

SPINOSAURUS

Spinosaurus had a **LARGE SAIL** that stood on its **BACK**.

TIME PERIOD LIVED: MIDDLE CRETACEOUS
100 MILLION YEARS AGO

LOCATION: EGYPT AND MOROCCO

LENGTH: 15 METRES (50 FEET)

A LONG SNOUT AND **CONE-SHAPED TEETH** HELPED IT TO CATCH FISH TO EAT.

SUCHOMIMUS

Suchomimus was a **FIERCE** meat-eater with **122 TEETH.**

THAT'S **FOUR TIMES AS MANY TEETH AS A HUMAN!**

12

TALL SPINES shot upwards from Acrocanthosaurus' **BACK.**

The spines may have formed a **SAIL** or supported a **HUMP OF MUSCLE.**

SAIL or HUMP OF MUSCLE?

ACROCANTHOSAURUS

TIME PERIOD LIVED: EARLY CRETACEOUS 110 MILLION YEARS AGO

LOCATION: UNITED STATES

LENGTH: 12 METRES (39 FEET)

ALLOSAURUS WEIGHED AROUND 2 TONNES!

That's about the SAME SIZE as a HIPPOPOTAMUS.

ALLOSAURUS

TIME PERIOD LIVED: LATE JURASSIC 150 MILLION YEARS AGO

LOCATION: NORTH AMERICA

LENGTH: 12 METRES (39 FEET)

CARCHARODONTOSAURUS HAD **LARGE TEETH WITH** BUMPS CALLED **SERRATIONS.**

THEY COULD CUT THROUGH MEAT LIKE A STEAK KNIFE!

CARCHARODONTOSAURUS

TIME PERIOD LIVED: MIDDLE CRETACEOUS 100 MILLION YEARS AGO

LOCATION: ALGERIA, EGYPT, MOROCCO AND NIGER

LENGTH: 12 METRES (40 FEET)

Wait, is that a
HAIRSTYLE?

NO! Cryolophosaurus had a **SIDEWAYS CREST** on top of its head.

CRYOLOPHOSAURUS

TIME PERIOD LIVED: EARLY JURASSIC 190 MILLION YEARS AGO

LOCATION: ANTARCTICA

LENGTH: 6 METRES (20 FEET)

A GIGANOTOSAURUS' SKULL WAS 1.5 METRES (5 FEET) LONG.

But its BRAIN was only the size of a BANANA!

GIGANOTOSAURUS

TIME PERIOD LIVED: MIDDLE CRETACEOUS 100 MILLION YEARS AGO

LOCATION: ARGENTINA

LENGTH: 12.5 METRES (41 FEET)

NEOVENATOR

TIME PERIOD LIVED: EARLY CRETACEOUS
130 MILLION YEARS AGO

LOCATION: UK

LENGTH: 7 METRES (23 FEET)

ONE NEOVENATOR
SKELETON HAD BROKEN
BONES IN ITS TAIL,
RIBCAGE AND SHOULDER.

IT MAY HAVE BROKEN
BONES DURING BRUTAL
FIGHTS WITH OTHER
DINOSAURS.

18

ALBERTOSAURUS
PROBABLY HUNTED
IN PACKS.

PALAEONTOLOGISTS
FOUND A GROUP OF
26 ALBERTOSAURUS,
INCLUDING ADULTS,
TEENAGERS AND BABIES.

ALBERTOSAURUS

TIME PERIOD LIVED: LATE CRETACEOUS
70 MILLION YEARS AGO

LOCATION: UNITED STATES AND CANADA

LENGTH: 8.5 METRES (28 FEET)

ALIORAMUS

TIME PERIOD LIVED: LATE CRETACEOUS
70 MILLION YEARS AGO

LOCATION: MONGOLIA

LENGTH: 5.8 METRES (19 FEET)

Alioramus had FIVE HORNS on top of its snout.

WHAT A SHOW-OFF!

COELURUS

TIME PERIOD LIVED: LATE JURASSIC
155 MILLION YEARS AGO

LOCATION: UNITED STATES

LENGTH: 2.5 METRES (8 FEET)

Coelurus had **LONG, THIN FINGERS** and a **LONG TAIL.**

IT WAS A FAST RUNNER AND **HUNTED SMALL ANIMALS.**

COMPSOGNATHUS

TIME PERIOD LIVED: **LATE JURASSIC**
150 MILLION YEARS AGO

LOCATION: **GERMANY AND FRANCE**

LENGTH: **1.2 METRES (4 FEET)**

Compsognathus
was a **FAST RUNNER**
and hunted
LIZARDS and **BUGS.**

ONE FOSSIL HAD
THE SKELETON OF
A LIZARD IN ITS
STOMACH.

DASPLETOSAURUS

Daspletosaurus **DID NOT** always get along together.

TIME PERIOD LIVED: LATE CRETACEOUS
80 MILLION YEARS AGO

LOCATION: UNITED STATES AND CANADA

LENGTH: 9 METRES (30 FEET)

MANY DASPLETOSAURUS FOSSILS HAVE HEALED INJURIES, SHOWING THAT THESE DINOS BIT EACH OTHER'S NOSES!

NOT ALL TYRANNOSAURS WERE GIANTS.

Eotyrannus was about the size of a LARGE DOG.

EOTYRANNUS

TIME PERIOD LIVED: EARLY CRETACEOUS 130 MILLION YEARS AGO

LOCATION: UK

LENGTH: 4.6 METRES (15 FEET)

GUANLONG

TIME PERIOD LIVED: LATE JURASSIC
160 MILLION YEARS AGO

LOCATION: CHINA

LENGTH: 3 METRES (9.8 FEET)

GUANLONG CAUSED QUITE A "FLAP" WHEN IT WAS DISCOVERED.

IT WAS ONE OF THE FIRST TYRANNOSAURS FOUND WITH FEATHERS!

TYRANNOSAURUS REX HAD THE STRONGEST BITE OF ANY LAND ANIMAL THAT EVER LIVED.

Its teeth were SERRATED like STEAK KNIVES. Each tooth was up to 30.5 CENTIMETRES (12 inches) LONG!

TYRANNOSAURUS REX

TIME PERIOD LIVED: LATE CRETACEOUS 70 MILLION YEARS AGO

LOCATION: NORTH AMERICA

LENGTH: 12 METRES (39 FEET)

DEINOCHEIRUS

Deinocheirus had a **DUCK-LIKE BILL,** a **SAIL** on its back and a **HUGE BELLY.**

TIME PERIOD LIVED: LATE CRETACEOUS 71 TO 69 MILLION YEARS AGO

LOCATION: MONGOLIA

LENGTH: 10 METRES (32.8 FEET)

IT DEFENDED ITSELF WITH **BIG CLAWS** ON ITS FEET.

GALLIMIMUS
MEANS
"CHICKEN MIMIC".

A fully grown
Gallimimus
weighed **HALF
A TONNE**.

THAT'S SOME CHICKEN!

GALLIMIMUS

**TIME PERIOD LIVED: LATE CRETACEOUS
70 MILLION YEARS AGO**

LOCATION: MONGOLIA

LENGTH: 6 METRES (20 FEET)

ORNITHOMIMUS

TIME PERIOD LIVED: LATE CRETACEOUS
65 MILLION YEARS AGO

LOCATION: UNITED STATES AND CANADA

LENGTH: 3 METRES (9.8 FEET)

ORNITHOMIMUS WAS COVERED IN FEATHERS.

It had long, WING-LIKE FEATHERS on its ARMS and a BEAK instead of teeth.

Like a modern mole, tiny Shuvuuia had **SHORT, STRONG ARMS** for **DIGGING.**

BUT SHUVUUIA HAD LONG, LIGHT LEGS FOR RUNNING, LIKE A ROADRUNNER'S LEGS.

SHUVUUIA

TIME PERIOD LIVED: LATE CRETACEOUS 86 TO 70 MILLION YEARS AGO

LOCATION: MONGOLIA

LENGTH: 60 CENTIMETRES (2 FEET)

BAMBIRAPTOR MAY HAVE CLIMBED TREES.

It also may have CURLED UP UNDER its FEATHERS to SLEEP.

BAMBIRAPTOR

TIME PERIOD LIVED: LATE CRETACEOUS 75 MILLION YEARS AGO

LOCATION: NORTH AMERICA

LENGTH: 1 METRE (3.3 FEET)

BUITRERAPTOR

The **TINY** Buitreraptor only **WEIGHED** 2.7 KILOGRAMS (6 POUNDS).

TIME PERIOD LIVED: LATE CRETACEOUS 90 MILLION YEARS AGO

LOCATION: ARGENTINA

LENGTH: 1.3 METRES (4 FEET)

THAT'S ABOUT THE SAME AS A CHIHUAHUA.

DEINONYCHUS

DEINONYCHUS TORE PREY WITH ITS **LONG CLAWS** AND **SHARP TEETH.**

TIME PERIOD LIVED: EARLY CRETACEOUS 118 TO 110 MILLION YEARS AGO

LOCATION: UNITED STATES

LENGTH: 3 METRES (9.8 FEET)

They probably worked together **IN PACKS** to bring down **LARGER DINOSAURS.**

Some species of Microraptor had long, **WING-LIKE** feathers on both its **ARMS** and **LEGS.**

MICRORAPTOR

THESE FEATHERS MAY HAVE HELPED THE MICRORAPTOR TO GLIDE FROM **TREE TO TREE.**

TIME PERIOD LIVED: EARLY CRETACEOUS 125 TO 122 MILLION YEARS AGO

LOCATION: CHINA

LENGTH: 80 CENTIMETRES (2.6 FEET)

TROODON MEANS "WOUNDING TOOTH".

TROODON

It had a very **BIG BRAIN** for its size and may have been the **CLEVEREST** of all dinosaurs.

TIME PERIOD LIVED: **LATE CRETACEOUS 74 TO 65 MILLION YEARS AGO**

LOCATION: **UNITED STATES AND CANADA**

LENGTH: **3 METRES (9.8 FEET)**

VELOCIRAPTOR

TIME PERIOD LIVED: LATE CRETACEOUS
75 MILLION YEARS AGO

LOCATION: ASIA

LENGTH: 1.8 METRES (5.9 FEET)

Velociraptor became popular after being featured in the **JURASSIC PARK** films.

VELOCIRAPTORS WERE ABOUT THE SIZE OF MODERN TURKEYS.

But in the films the **VELOCIRAPTORS** were based on the much larger **DEINONYCHUS** and **UTAHRAPTOR**.

YAVERLANDIA WAS ONE CLEVER DINO!

It had a **LARGE BRAIN** in its domed head.

YAVERLANDIA

TIME PERIOD LIVED: EARLY CRETACEOUS
130 TO 125 MILLION YEARS AGO

LOCATION: UK

LENGTH: 3 METRES (10 FEET)

Avimimus was so similar to a BIRD that palaeontologists mistook it for a BIRD at first.

AVIMIMUS

TIME PERIOD LIVED: LATE CRETACEOUS 80 TO 75 MILLION YEARS AGO

LOCATION: CHINA AND MONGOLIA

LENGTH: 1.5 METRES (4.9 FEET)

FOR PROTECTION AGAINST PREDATORS, AVIMIMUS LIVED IN LARGE HERDS.

BEIPIAOSAURUS

TIME PERIOD LIVED: EARLY CRETACEOUS
127 TO 121 MILLION YEARS AGO

LOCATION: CHINA

LENGTH: 2 METRES (6.7 FEET)

For a long time, the only dinosaurs found with **FEATHERS** were **TINY** and very similar to **BIRDS**.

Beipiaosaurus changed that – it was the size of a **SMALL BEAR**.

The name Caudipteryx means "TAIL WING" or "TAIL FEATHERS".

CAUDIPTERYX

IT WAS THE FIRST DINOSAUR TO BE FOUND WITH A BIG FAN OF TAIL FEATHERS, LIKE A TURKEY.

TIME PERIOD LIVED: EARLY CRETACEOUS 125 TO 122 MILLION YEARS AGO

LOCATION: CHINA

LENGTH: 1 METRE (3.3 FEET)

FALCARIUS

TIME PERIOD LIVED: EARLY CRETACEOUS
125 MILLION YEARS AGO

LOCATION: UNITED STATES

LENGTH: 4 METRES (13 FEET)

FALCARIUS WAS RELATED TO CARNIVORES SUCH AS ALLOSAURUS AND T. REX.

BUT IT EVOLVED TO EAT PLANTS, NOT MEAT!

INCISIVOSAURUS

INCISIVOSAURUS HAD BIG FRONT TEETH FOR CUTTING PLANTS, LIKE A BEAVER OR A RABBIT.

Protarchaeopteryx
looked a lot like a bird,
BUT IT COULD NOT FLY.

Long, **FEATHERED
ARMS** extended from
its small, feathered body.

PROTARCHAEOPTERYX

TIME PERIOD LIVED: **EARLY CRETACEOUS
125 TO 113 MILLION YEARS AGO**

LOCATION: **CHINA**

LENGTH: **2 METRES (6.7 FEET)**

Therizinosaurus
had the
LONGEST CLAWS
of any dinosaur.

THEY WERE
NEARLY 1 METRE
(3.3 FEET) LONG!

THERIZINOSAURUS

TIME PERIOD LIVED: LATE CRETACEOUS
70 MILLION YEARS AGO

LOCATION: MONGOLIA

LENGTH: 10 METRES (33 FEET)

EFRAASIA

TIME PERIOD LIVED: LATE TRIASSIC 210 MILLION YEARS AGO

LOCATION: EUROPE

LENGTH: 6 METRES (20 FEET)

Efraasia was a HERBIVORE – it ATE PLANTS.

IT WALKED ON TWO LEGS AND USED ITS FRONT TEETH TO SCRAPE LEAVES FROM TREES.

PLATEOSAURUS

TIME PERIOD LIVED: LATE TRIASSIC 210 MILLION YEARS AGO

LOCATION: EUROPE

LENGTH: 7-9 METRES (23-30 FEET)

PLATEOSAURUS WAS A GIANT! IT WEIGHED ALMOST 4 TONNES.

Sometimes WHOLE HERDS of these heavy dinosaurs would get TRAPPED IN MUD.

Their skeletons were preserved and were later DISCOVERED TOGETHER.

Saturnalia had a **LONG TAIL** that it used to **TURN QUICKLY** when running.

SATURNALIA

LIKE AN IGUANA, IT ATE PLANTS USING ITS LEAF-SHAPED TEETH.

TIME PERIOD LIVED: LATE TRIASSIC 225 MILLION YEARS AGO

LOCATION: BRAZIL AND ZIMBABWE

LENGTH: 1.5 METRES (5 FEET)

THECODONTOSAURUS

TIME PERIOD LIVED: LATE TRIASSIC
210 MILLION YEARS AGO

LOCATION: UK

LENGTH: 2 METRES (7 FEET)

THECODONTOSAURUS WAS ONE OF THE EARLIEST LONG-NECKED DINOSAURS TO EXIST ON EARTH.

It was also one of the FIRST dinosaurs to be DISCOVERED.

In 1836, it became only the FIFTH dinosaur ever to be NAMED.

APATOSAURUS
WEIGHED
ABOUT 32 TONNES!

APATOSAURUS

TIME PERIOD LIVED: LATE JURASSIC
150 MILLION YEARS AGO

LOCATION: NORTH AMERICA

LENGTH: 21 METRES (69 FEET)

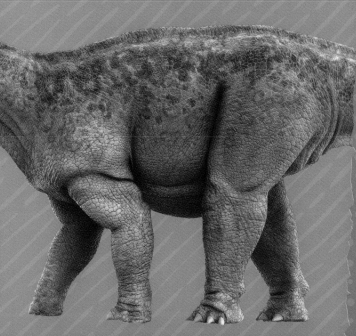

That's the
weight of about
FIVE AFRICAN
ELEPHANTS!

LONG FRONT LEGS HELPED BRACHIOSAURUS TO EAT LEAVES FROM TALL TREES.

Brachiosaurus was 14 METRES (45 feet) TALL!

BRACHIOSAURUS

That's more than 4 STOREYS HIGH!

TIME PERIOD LIVED: LATE JURASSIC 150 MILLION YEARS AGO

LOCATION: NORTH AMERICA

LENGTH: 30 METRES (98 FEET)

BRACHYTRACHELOPAN

Brachytrachelopan had a built-in WEAPON – a LONG TAIL it could use as a WHIP!

TIME PERIOD LIVED: LATE JURASSIC 150 MILLION YEARS AGO

LOCATION: ARGENTINA

LENGTH: 11 METRES (35 FEET)

ITS NECK WAS JUST 1.5 METRES (5 FEET) LONG.

CAMARASAURUS

TIME PERIOD LIVED: LATE JURASSIC 150 TO 145 MILLION YEARS AGO

LOCATION: UNITED STATES

LENGTH: 15 METRES (50 FEET)

SCIENTISTS HAVE FOUND BONES OF A BABY CAMARASAURUS THAT HAD **NOT YET HATCHED** OUT OF ITS EGG.

DIPLODOCUS

TIME PERIOD LIVED: LATE JURASSIC
150 MILLION YEARS AGO

LOCATION: NORTH AMERICA

LENGTH: 27 METRES (90 FEET)

Diplodocus was one
of the LIGHTEST
large dinosaurs.

It didn't weigh
much more than a big
ELEPHANT.

53

HUABEISAURUS

TIME PERIOD LIVED: **LATE CRETACEOUS 75 MILLION YEARS AGO**

LOCATION: **CHINA**

LENGTH: **17 METRES (55 FEET)**

HUABEISAURUS HAD **AIR-FILLED HOLES** IN ITS BACKBONE.

The pattern of the **HOLES** helps **SCIENTISTS** to tell Huabeisaurus **APART** from its **RELATIVES**.

Omeisaurus' **NECK** was **9 METRES** (30 feet) **LONG.**

OMEISAURUS

THAT'S THE LENGTH OF AN AVERAGE-SIZED HOUSE!

TIME PERIOD LIVED: LATE JURASSIC 169 TO 159 MILLION YEARS AGO

LOCATION: CHINA

LENGTH: 9 METRES (30 FEET)

SUUWASSEA

TIME PERIOD LIVED: LATE JURASSIC 156 TO 151 MILLION YEARS AGO

LOCATION: UNITED STATES

LENGTH: 15 METRES (50 FEET)

SUUWASSEA'S TEETH WERE SHAPED LIKE PENCILS.

This dinosaur used its TEETH to STRIP LEAVES from BRANCHES.

AMPELOSAURUS HAD BONY ARMOUR IN ITS SKIN.

THE LARGEST PIECES OF ARMOUR WERE THE SIZE OF DINNER PLATES!

AMPELOSAURUS

TIME PERIOD LIVED: **LATE CRETACEOUS 70 MILLION YEARS AGO**

LOCATION: **FRANCE**

LENGTH: **15 METRES (50 FEET)**

ARGENTINOSAURUS

TIME PERIOD LIVED: MIDDLE CRETACEOUS
100 MILLION YEARS AGO

LOCATION: ARGENTINA

LENGTH: 30 METRES (100 FEET)

ARGENTINOSAURUS
IS STILL THE
LARGEST KNOWN
DINOSAUR.

That's the
distance from
the FLOOR TO
THE CEILING
in many houses.

Its THIGH BONE
was just over
2.4 METRES
(8 FEET) LONG!

FUTALOGNKOSAURUS HAD HIPS ALMOST 3 METRES (10 FEET) WIDE!

IT ATE LEAVES FROM TREES IN TROPICAL FORESTS.

FUTALOGNKOSAURUS

TIME PERIOD LIVED: LATE CRETACEOUS 85 MILLION YEARS AGO

LOCATION: SOUTH AMERICA

LENGTH: 26 METRES (85 FEET)

MAGYAROSAURUS

TIME PERIOD LIVED: **LATE CRETACEOUS**
70 MILLION YEARS AGO

LOCATION: **ROMANIA**

LENGTH: **6 METRES (20 FEET)**

MAGYAROSAURUS HAD **BONY PLATES** COVERING ITS BACK.

IT WAS THE **SMALLEST** LONG-NECKED DINOSAUR **WITH ARMOUR.**

Paralititan was one of the **LARGEST DINOSAURS.**

IT WEIGHED NEARLY **70 TONNES!**

ITS FOSSIL WAS FOUND IN A MANGROVE SWAMP.

PARALITITAN

TIME PERIOD LIVED: MIDDLE CRETACEOUS 95 MILLION YEARS AGO

LOCATION: EGYPT

LENGTH: 30 METRES (100 FEET)

Saltasaurus was the FIRST long-necked dinosaur to be DISCOVERED with ARMOUR PLATES.

SALTASAURUS

TIME PERIOD LIVED: LATE CRETACEOUS 70 TO 65 MILLION YEARS AGO

LOCATION: ARGENTINA

LENGTH: 8 METRES (25 FEET)

GIGANTSPINOSAURUS

TIME PERIOD LIVED: LATE JURASSIC
160 MILLION YEARS AGO

LOCATION: CHINA

LENGTH: 4.6 METRES (15 FEET)

GIGANTSPINOSAURUS HAD HUGE SPIKES ON ITS SHOULDERS.

THIS DINO PROBABLY USED ITS SPIKES FOR PROTECTION AND FOR SHOWING OFF.

63

HESPEROSAURUS

TIME PERIOD LIVED: LATE JURASSIC
150 MILLION YEARS AGO

LOCATION: UNITED STATES

LENGTH: 6 METRES (20 FEET)

WIDE PLATES COVERED HESPEROSAURUS' BACK.

SCIENTISTS USE THE SHAPE OF THE PLATES TO TELL HESPEROSAURUS AND STEGOSAURUS APART.

Like a **SPIDER CRAB**,
Huayangosaurus
had **BONY PLATES** and
SPIKES for **PROTECTION**.

HUAYANGOSAURUS

TIME PERIOD LIVED: MIDDLE JURASSIC
165 MILLION YEARS AGO

LOCATION: CHINA

LENGTH: 4.5 METRES (14.8 FEET)

KENTROSAURUS

Kentrosaurus had **SMALL PLATES** on its **NECK** and **BODY**.

TIME PERIOD LIVED: **LATE JURASSIC 150 MILLION YEARS AGO**

LOCATION: **TANZANIA**

LENGTH: **5 METRES (16 FEET)**

SPIKES SHOT UP FROM ITS SHOULDERS AND LINED ITS TAIL.

LEXOVISAURUS IS ONE OF THE FEW PLATED DINOSAURS FROM EUROPE.

PALAEONTOLOGISTS HAVE FOUND ONLY A FEW OF ITS BONES.

SO NO ONE IS SURE WHAT THIS DINOSAUR LOOKED LIKE.

LEXOVISAURUS

TIME PERIOD LIVED: MIDDLE JURASSIC 165 MILLION YEARS AGO

LOCATION: UK AND FRANCE

LENGTH: 1.5 METRES (5 FEET)

STEGOSAURUS

TIME PERIOD LIVED: LATE JURASSIC 150 MILLION YEARS AGO

LOCATION: NORTH AMERICA

LENGTH: 8 METRES (25 FEET)

STEGOSAURUS HAD LARGE PLATES POINTING OUT OF ITS BACK.

THE SHARP SPIKES ON ITS TAIL COULD BE USED FOR DEFENCE.

TUOJIANGOSAURUS

TIME PERIOD LIVED: LATE JURASSIC
160 MILLION YEARS AGO

LOCATION: CHINA

LENGTH: 7 METRES (23 FEET)

Tuojiangosaurus had NARROW back plates and SHARP shoulder spikes.

Much like a PORCUPINE, Tuojiangosaurus SCARED OFF predators with its SPIKES.

69

YINGSHANOSAURUS

Yingshanosaurus had **VERY SMALL PLATES**, only **15 CENTIMETRES (6 inches) TALL.**

By comparison, Stegosaurus' plates were **FOUR TIMES AS BIG!**

TIME PERIOD LIVED: LATE JURASSIC 155 MILLION YEARS AGO

LOCATION: CHINA

LENGTH: 5 METRES (16 FEET)

THE FIRST ALETOPELTA TO BE DISCOVERED HAD DIED AND FLOATED OUT TO SEA.

SHARKS CHOMPED ON ITS BONES.

ALETOPELTA

TIME PERIOD LIVED: LATE CRETACEOUS
70 MILLION YEARS AGO

LOCATION: NORTH AMERICA

LENGTH: 5 METRES (16 FEET)

LIKE OTHER ARMOURED DINOS, ANKYLOSAURUS HAD PLATES COVERED BY A LAYER OF KERATIN.

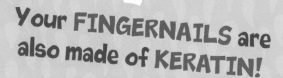

Your FINGERNAILS are also made of KERATIN!

ANKYLOSAURUS

TIME PERIOD LIVED: LATE CRETACEOUS 65 MILLION YEARS AGO

LOCATION: NORTH AMERICA

LENGTH: 7 METRES (23 FEET)

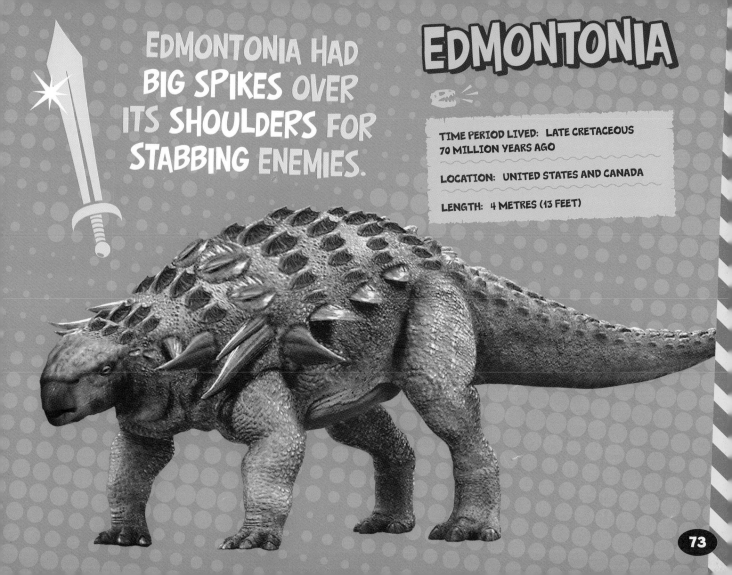

EDMONTONIA HAD **BIG SPIKES** OVER ITS **SHOULDERS** FOR **STABBING** ENEMIES.

EDMONTONIA

TIME PERIOD LIVED: LATE CRETACEOUS 70 MILLION YEARS AGO

LOCATION: UNITED STATES AND CANADA

LENGTH: 4 METRES (13 FEET)

EUOPLOCEPHALUS

Euoplocephalus means
"WELL-ARMOURED HEAD".

It had a ring of
ARMOUR around
its **NECK**, like a
BONY COLLAR.

THIS DINOSAUR
EVEN HAD
ARMOUR PLATES
IN ITS EYELIDS!

GASTONIA

TIME PERIOD LIVED: EARLY CRETACEOUS
129 TO 125 MILLION YEARS AGO

LOCATION: NORTH AMERICA

LENGTH: 4.6 METRES (15 FEET)

Gastonia had TOUGH PLATES and SPIKES on its BODY.

WHEN THREATENED, THIS DINO WOULD CROUCH LOW TO THE GROUND.

75

Minmi's BACK was PROTECTED with PLATES, and its HIPS and TAIL had SPIKES.

MINMI

IT IS NAMED AFTER MINMI'S CROSSING IN AUSTRALIA.

The **BRAIN** of Pawpawsaurus was **10 CENTIMETRES** (4 inches) **LONG** and **2.5 CM** (1 inch) **WIDE**.

THAT'S ABOUT THE SIZE OF A GHERKIN!

PAWPAWSAURUS

TIME PERIOD LIVED: MIDDLE CRETACEOUS 100 MILLION YEARS AGO

LOCATION: UNITED STATES

LENGTH: 4 METRES (13 FEET)

POLACANTHUS

TIME PERIOD LIVED: EARLY CRETACEOUS 130 MILLION YEARS AGO

LOCATION: WESTERN EUROPE

LENGTH: 5 METRES (16 FEET)

POLACANTHUS, FROM EUROPE, WAS A CLOSE RELATIVE OF GASTONIA, FROM NORTH AMERICA.

NORTH AMERICA

EUROPE

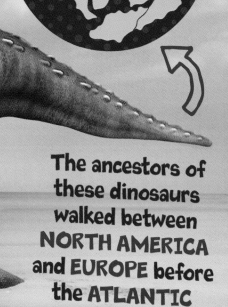

The ancestors of these dinosaurs walked between **NORTH AMERICA** and **EUROPE** before the **ATLANTIC OCEAN** opened up.

SCUTELLOSAURUS

TIME PERIOD LIVED: EARLY JURASSIC
195 MILLION YEARS AGO

LOCATION: UNITED STATES

LENGTH: 1.2 METRES (3.9 FEET)

Scutellosaurus had more than 300 ARMOUR PLATES, but it was only about the size of a DOG!

STRUTHIOSAURUS

TIME PERIOD LIVED: LATE CRETACEOUS
65 MILLION YEARS AGO

LOCATION: AUSTRIA, FRANCE AND ROMANIA

LENGTH: 2.5 METRES (8.2 FEET)

STRUTHIOSAURUS WAS SMALL – ONLY ABOUT THE SIZE OF A SOFA.

IT LIVED ON AN ISLAND WITH OTHER DWARF DINOSAURS.

Tiny **GASPARINISAURA** was **ONLY** as **BIG** as a **DOMESTIC CAT!**

But it **LIVED** alongside Argentinosaurus, **THE LARGEST DINOSAUR EVER DISCOVERED.**

GASPARINISAURA

TIME PERIOD LIVED: LATE CRETACEOUS
83 TO 78 MILLION YEARS AGO

LOCATION: ARGENTINA

LENGTH: 80 CENTIMETRES (2.6 FEET)

Hypsilophodon had **TEETH** that **SLID AGAINST** each other like **SCISSORS**.

The **SLIDING MOTION** kept the teeth **SHARP** for **CUTTING UP** leaves and twigs.

HYPSILOPHODON

TIME PERIOD LIVED: **EARLY CRETACEOUS 130 TO 125 MILLION YEARS AGO**

LOCATION: **EUROPE**

LENGTH: **2.3 METRES (7.5 FEET)**

IGUANODON

TIME PERIOD LIVED: EARLY CRETACEOUS
130 MILLION YEARS AGO

LOCATION: EUROPE

LENGTH: 10 METRES (33 FEET)

THUMB

LIKE OTHER BIRD-FOOT
DINOSAURS, IGUANODON
HAD LEAF-SHAPED TEETH
FOR EATING PLANTS.

ITS HANDS EACH
HAD FOUR FINGERS
AND A SHARP SPIKE
FOR A THUMB.

Leaellynasaura had **LARGE EYES** and a **BIG BRAIN.**

Its **TAIL** was **THREE TIMES** as **LONG** as its **BODY!**

LEAELLYNASAURA

TIME PERIOD LIVED: EARLY CRETACEOUS 112 TO 104 MILLION YEARS AGO

LOCATION: AUSTRALIA

LENGTH: 1 METRE (3.3 FEET)

MUTTABURRASAURUS

MUTTABURRASAURUS HAD A BUMP ON ITS NOSE.

THE BUMP MAY HAVE HAVE BEEN A BRIGHT COLOUR TO ATTRACT OTHER DINOSAURS.

ORYCTODROMEUS

ORYCTODROMEUS WAS THE **FIRST DINOSAUR** DISCOVERED **INSIDE** A BURROW!

TIME PERIOD LIVED: MIDDLE CRETACEOUS 95 MILLION YEARS AGO

LOCATION: UNITED STATES

LENGTH: 2.1 METRES (7 FEET)

Edmontosaurus had teeth that **LOCKED TOGETHER** to make a **HARD, GRINDING SURFACE.**

The grinding teeth helped Edmontosaurus to **CHEW LEAVES** and **FRUIT.**

EDMONTOSAURUS

TIME PERIOD LIVED: LATE CRETACEOUS 70 MILLION YEARS AGO

LOCATION: CANADA AND THE UNITED STATES

LENGTH: 9 METRES (30 FEET)

HADROSAURUS WAS THE FIRST DINOSAUR DISCOVERED IN NORTH AMERICA.

IT WAS ALSO THE FIRST DINOSAUR TO HAVE ITS SKELETON PUT ON DISPLAY IN A MUSEUM.

HADROSAURUS

TIME PERIOD LIVED: LATE CRETACEOUS 79 MILLION YEARS AGO

LOCATION: UNITED STATES

LENGTH: 7 METRES (23 FEET)

FOSSILS of Maiasaura
EGGS, YOUNG Maiasaura
and ADULT Maiasaura
have been FOUND
IN NESTS.

Fossils show that
NEWLY HATCHED
Maiasaura COULD NOT
WALK straight away.

MAIASAURA

TIME PERIOD LIVED: LATE CRETACEOUS
80 TO 75 MILLION YEARS AGO

LOCATION: UNITED STATES

LENGTH: 7 METRES (23 FEET)

SAUROLOPHUS

TIME PERIOD LIVED: LATE CRETACEOUS 70 TO 65 MILLION YEARS AGO

LOCATION: MONGOLIA AND CANADA

LENGTH: 8.2 METRES (27 FEET)

Most duckbills could **BLOW AIR** through their **CRESTS** to make **NOISES.**

But Saurolophus had a crest made of **SOLID BONE.**

SHANTUNGOSAURUS

TIME PERIOD LIVED: LATE CRETACEOUS
78 TO 74 MILLION YEARS AGO

LOCATION: CHINA

LENGTH: 15.2 METRES (50 FEET)

SHANTUNGOSAURUS WAS LARGER THAN T. REX!

ITS SKULL WAS MORE THAN 1.5 METRES (5 FEET) LONG.

TSINTAOSAURUS

TIME PERIOD LIVED: LATE CRETACEOUS
84 TO 71 MILLION YEARS AGO

LOCATION: CHINA

LENGTH: 8.2 METRES (27 FEET)

The first Tsintaosaurus fossils found included a SKULL with a SPIKE on its FOREHEAD.

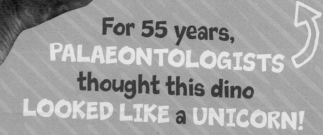

For 55 years, PALAEONTOLOGISTS thought this dino LOOKED LIKE a UNICORN!

Then in 2013, a more COMPLETE SKULL showed that Tsintaosaurus had a FAN-SHAPED CREST, not a SPIKE.

MICROPACHYCEPHALOSAURUS

TIME PERIOD LIVED: LATE CRETACEOUS 70 MILLION YEARS AGO

LOCATION: CHINA

LENGTH: 1 METRE (3.3 FEET)

MICROPACHYCEPHALOSAURUS WAS SMALL ...

...BUT IT WAS GIVEN THE LONGEST NAME OF ANY DINOSAUR.

Pachycephalosaurus means "THICK-HEADED LIZARD".

The dome on its SKULL was SOLID BONE – 25 centimetres (10 inches) thick!

PACHYCEPHALOSAURUS

TIME PERIOD LIVED: LATE CRETACEOUS
65 MILLION YEARS AGO

LOCATION: UNITED STATES

LENGTH: 8 METRES (26 FEET)

ARCHAEOCERATOPS

TIME PERIOD LIVED: MIDDLE CRETACEOUS
99 MILLION YEARS AGO

LOCATION: CHINA

LENGTH: 1.3 METRES (4.3 FEET)

Archaeoceratops was one of the EARLIEST "HORNED DINOSAURS"– but it DIDN'T ACTUALLY HAVE ANY HORNS!

IT HAD A LARGE HEAD WITH A BEAK AND A FRILL, AND IT WALKED ON TWO LEGS INSTEAD OF FOUR.

MONTANACERATOPS

TIME PERIOD LIVED: LATE TRIASSIC
228 MILLION YEARS AGO

LOCATION: UNITED STATES AND CANADA

LENGTH: 3 METRES (10 FEET)

For decades, scientists thought Montanaceratops had a **SMALL HORN** on its **NOSE.**

THEN THEY REALIZED THE "HORN" WAS REALLY PART OF THE DINOSAUR'S CHEEK!

NEDOCERATOPS

TIME PERIOD LIVED: LATE CRETACEOUS
70 MILLION YEARS AGO

LOCATION: UNITED STATES

LENGTH: 7 METRES (23 FEET)

NEDOCERATOPS
IS ON ITS
THIRD NAME!

HELLO
MY NAME IS

NEDOCERATOPS

1. WHEN IT WAS FIRST DISCOVERED, IT WAS NAMED **DICERATOPS**.

2. THEN FOR A LONG TIME, SCIENTISTS THOUGHT IT WAS JUST AN UNUSUAL **TRICERATOPS**.

3. FINALLY, IN 2007 IT WAS GIVEN THE NEW NAME, **NEDOCERATOPS**.

PACHYRHINOSAURUS

TIME PERIOD LIVED: LATE CRETACEOUS 70 MILLION YEARS AGO

LOCATION: UNITED STATES AND CANADA

LENGTH: 6 METRES (20 FEET)

PALAEONTOLOGISTS HAVE FOUND BONEBEDS WITH THOUSANDS OF PACHYRHINOSAURUS FOSSILS.

THESE FOSSILS SHOW THAT PACHYRHINOSAURUS LIVED IN BIG HERDS, JUST LIKE BISON AND WILDEBEEST TODAY.

PROTOCERATOPS

Scientists **KNOW MORE** about Protoceratops than almost **ANY OTHER DINOSAUR.**

TIME PERIOD LIVED: LATE CRETACEOUS 70 MILLION YEARS AGO

LOCATION: ASIA

LENGTH: 1.8 METRES (5.9 FEET)

Nests full of babies show that **PROTOCERATOPS PARENTS CARED FOR THEIR YOUNG.**

STYRACOSAURUS

TIME PERIOD LIVED: LATE CRETACEOUS
75 MILLION YEARS AGO

LOCATION: NORTH AMERICA

LENGTH: 5.5 METRES (18 FEET)

Styracosaurus had a **FAN** of **SPIKES** on the back of its **FRILL**.

A LARGE HORN STUCK OUT FROM ITS NOSE.

TOROSAURUS

TIME PERIOD LIVED: LATE CRETACEOUS
66 MILLION YEARS AGO

LOCATION: NORTH AMERICA

LENGTH: 7.5 METRES (25 FEET)

THE **SKULL** OF TOROSAURUS WAS 2.7 METRES (9 FEET) LONG!

THAT'S TWICE AS LONG AS THE **SKULL** OF A T.REX!

TRICERATOPS

TIME PERIOD LIVED: LATE CRETACEOUS
70 MILLION YEARS AGO

LOCATION: NORTH AMERICA

LENGTH: 9 METRES (30 FEET)

MANY TRICERATOPS
SKULLS HAVE HEALED WOUNDS
ON THEIR FRILLS FROM
OTHER TRICERATOPS ATTACKS.

Just like
SHEEP, ANTELOPE
and BISON today, these
dinosaurs used their
horns to fight!

TRUE BIRDS

8. PLANT-EATING RAPTORS

7. MEAT-EATING RAPTORS

6. BIRD-MIMICS

5. TYRANNOSAUR RELATIVES

4. ALLOSAUR RELATIVES

3. SPINOSAUR RELATIVES

2. BUMP-HEADED MEAT-EATERS

1. EARLY MEAT-EATERS

THEROPODS
(BIRD-LIKE DINOS)

CARNIVORES

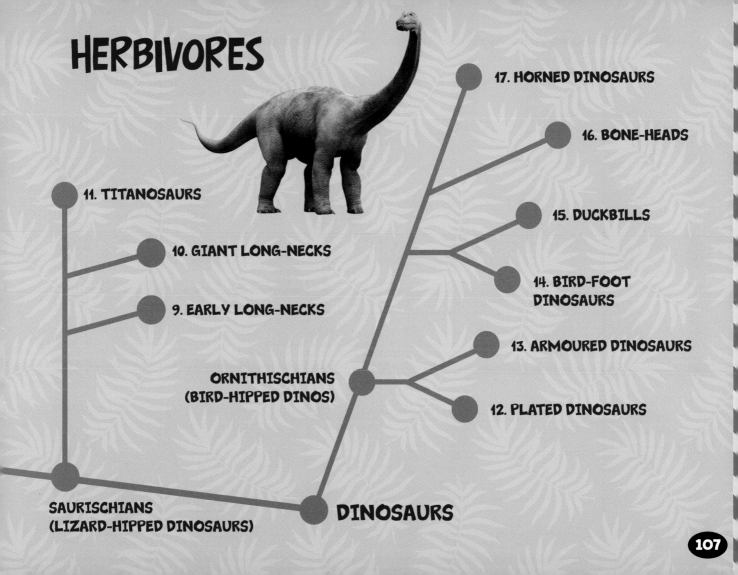

HERBIVORES

11. TITANOSAURS

10. GIANT LONG-NECKS

9. EARLY LONG-NECKS

ORNITHISCHIANS
(BIRD-HIPPED DINOS)

SAURISCHIANS
(LIZARD-HIPPED DINOSAURS)

DINOSAURS

17. HORNED DINOSAURS

16. BONE-HEADS

15. DUCKBILLS

14. BIRD-FOOT
DINOSAURS

13. ARMOURED DINOSAURS

12. PLATED DINOSAURS

DINOSAUR TIMELINE

	1. EARLY MEAT-EATERS	2. BUMP-HEADED MEAT-EATERS	3. SPINOSAUR RELATIVES	4. ALLOSAUR RELATIVES	5. TYRANNOSAUR RELATIVES	6. BIRD-MIMICS	7. MEAT-EATING RAPTORS	8. PLANT-EATING RAPTORS
LATE TRIASSIC	Coelophysis Eoraptor Herrerasaurus Liliensternus							
EARLY JURASSIC				Cryolophosaurus				
MIDDLE JURASSIC								
LATE JURASSIC				Allosaurus	Coelurus Compsognathus Guanlong			
EARLY CRETACEOUS			Baryonyx Suchomimus	Acrocanthosaurus Neovenator	Eotyrannus		Deinonychus Microraptor Yaverlandia	Beipiaosaurus Caudipteryx Falcarius Incisivosaurus Protarchaeopteryx
MIDDLE CRETACEOUS		Rugops	Spinosaurus	Carcharodontosaurus Giganotosaurus				
LATE CRETACEOUS		Carnotaurus Dahalokely Masiakasaurus			Albertosaurus Alioramus Daspletosaurus Tyrannosaurus rex	Deinocheirus Gallimimus Ornithomimus Shuvuuia	Bambiraptor Buitreraptor Troodon Velociraptor	Avimimus Therizinosaurus

9. EARLY LONG-NECKS	10. GIANT LONG-NECKS	11. TITANOSAURS	12. PLATED DINOSAURS	13. ARMOURED DINOSAURS	14. BIRD-FOOT DINOSAURS	15. DUCKBILLS	16. BONE-HEADS	17. HORNED DINOSAURS
Efraasia Plateosaurus Saturnalia Thecodontosaurus								
				Scutellosaurus				
			Huayangosaurus Lexovisaurus					
	Apatosaurus Brachiosaurus Brachytrachelopan Camarasaurus Diplodocus Omeisaurus Suuwassea		Gigantspinosaurus Hesperosaurus Kentrosaurus Stegosaurus Tuojiangosaurus Yingshanosaurus					
				Gastonia Minmi Polacanthus	Hypsilophodon Iguanodon Leaellynasaura Muttaburrasaurus			
		Argentinosaurus Paralititan		Pawpawsaurus	Oryctodromeus			Archaeoceratops
Huabeisaurus		Ampelosaurus Futalognkosaurus Magyarosaurus Saltasaurus		Aletopelta Ankylosaurus Edmontonia Euoplocephalus Struthiosaurus	Gasparinisaura	Edmontosaurus Hadrosaurus Maiasaura Saurolophus Shantungosaurus Tsintaosaurus	Micropachycephalosaurus Pachycephalosaurus	Montanaceratops Nedoceratops Pachyrhinosaurus Protoceratops Styracosaurus Torosaurus Triceratops

GLOSSARY

attract   get the attention of someone or something

burrow   hole in the ground made or used by an animal

combat   fighting

crest   curved shape that sticks up from a dinosaur's head

decade   ten years

domed   rounded on top

fossil   remains or traces of an animal or plant, preserved as rock

herd   large group of animals that lives or moves together

hollow   empty on the inside

keratin   hard substance that forms hair and fingernails; dinosaur plates were also made of keratin

modern   up-to-date or new

navigate   steer a course

palaeontologist   scientist who studies fossils

plate   flat, bony growth

predator   animal that hunts other animals for food

preserve   protect something so it stays in its original state

sail   tall, thin, upright structure on the backs of some dinosaurs

spine   hard, sharp, pointed growth

BOOKS

Allosaurus vs Brachiosaurus: Might Against Height (Dinosaur Wars), Michael O'Hearn (Raintree, 2011)

Knowledge Encyclopedia Dinosaur! Over 60 Prehistoric Creatures as You've Never Seen Them Before, DK (DK Children, 2014)

Pocket Eyewitness Dinosaurs: Facts at Your Fingertips, DK (DK Children, 2018)

Worlds' Scariest Dinosaurs (Extreme Dinosaurs), Rupert Matthews (Raintree, 2012)

WEBSITES

Find out more about dinosaurs and prehistoric life.
www.dkfindout.com/uk/dinosaurs-and-prehistoric-life/

Use this pronunciation guide to hear how to say the names of your favourite dinos!
www.usborne.com/quicklinks/eng/catalogue/catalogue.aspx?loc=uk&id=6500

INDEX

Allosaur relatives 13–18
armour
  plates 57, 60, 62, 64, 65, 66, 67, 68,
    69, 70, 72, 74, 75, 76, 79
  spikes 63, 66, 68, 69, 73, 75, 76,
    102
armoured dinosaurs 71–80

beaks 29, 95
bills 27
bird-foot dinosaurs 81–86
bird-mimics 27–30
bite 26
bone-heads 93–94
bones 2, 3, 9, 18, 22, 54, 57, 58, 60,
    90, 94
brains 17, 35, 37, 77, 84
bump-headed meat-eaters 6–9

claws 5, 27, 33, 44
climbing 31
colours 85
crests 16, 90, 92

diet 2, 10, 11, 12, 21, 22, 33, 41, 45,
    47, 50, 56, 59, 83, 87
digging 30
dinosaur family tree 106–107
dinosaur timeline 108–109
duckbills 87–92

early long-necks 45–48
early meat-eaters 2–4
eggs 89
eyes 6, 84

feathers 25, 29, 31, 34, 39, 40, 43
feet 4, 83
fighting 18, 23, 51, 104
fingers 21, 83
fossils 2, 22, 23, 40, 46, 48, 52, 61,
    67, 71, 86, 88, 89, 92, 100
frills 95, 102, 104

giant long-necks 49–56

herds 38, 100
horned dinosaurs 95–105
horns 6, 20, 95, 97, 102
hunting 4, 5, 8, 11, 21, 22, 33

identification 54
intelligence 35, 37

jaws 10
jumping 34
Jurassic Park (films) 36

legs 50

meat-eating raptors 31–37

nests 101

packs 19
plant-eating raptors 38–44
plated dinosaurs 63–70

sails 11, 13, 27
scales 6
size 7, 14, 17, 24, 26, 28, 32, 36, 39,
    44, 50, 51, 55, 58, 59, 60, 61,
    70, 79, 80, 81, 84, 91, 93, 103
skin 57
skulls 9, 17, 91, 92, 94, 103, 104
snouts 11, 20
sounds 90
speed 3, 6, 22, 30, 47
spikes 83, 92
Spinosaur relatives 10–12

tails 21, 47, 51, 84
teeth 5, 8, 10, 11, 12, 15, 33, 35, 42,
    45, 47, 56, 82, 83, 87
  serrations 15, 26
titanosaurs 57–62
Tyrannosaur relatives 19–26

weight 3, 14, 46, 49, 53, 61

Raintree is an imprint of Capstone Global Library Limited, a company incorporated in England and Wales having its registered office at 264 Banbury Road, Oxford, OX2 7DY – Registered company number: 6695582

www.raintree.co.uk
myorders@raintree.co.uk

Text © Capstone Global Library Limited 2019
The moral rights of the proprietor have been asserted.

Original illustrations © Capstone Global Library Ltd
Originated by Capstone Global Library Ltd
Printed and bound in India

ISBN 978 1 4747 6289 2
22 21 20 19 18
10 9 8 7 6 5 4 3 2 1

British Library Cataloguing in Publication Data
A full catalogue record for this book is available from the British Library.

Acknowledgements
We would like to thank the following for permission to reproduce photographs: Shutterstock: Aaron Amat, 3 (stopwatch), azure1, 8 (fish), Studioimagen73, 10 (steak), J. Lekavicius, 14 (hippo), Ian 2010, 17 (banana), Lena Pan, 28 (chicken), Eric Isselee, 30 (mole), Eric Isselee, 32 (chihuahua), Christine C Brooks, 47 (iguana), catshila, 56 (pencils), Duda Vasilii, 57 (dinner plate), avarand, 65 (crab), Eric Isselee, 69 (porcupine), rangizzz, 72 (finger), domnitsky, 77 (pickle), outc, 82 (scissors), Macrovector, 85 (orange light)

Design Elements by Shutterstock, Getty Images and DynamoLimited

Every effort has been made to contact copyright holders of material reproduced in this book. Any omissions will be rectified in subsequent printings if notice is given to the publisher.

All the internet addresses (URLs) given in this book were valid at the time of going to press. However, due to the dynamic nature of the internet, some addresses may have changed, or sites may have changed or ceased to exist since publication. While the author and publisher regret any inconvenience this may cause readers, no responsibility for any such changes can be accepted by either the author or the publisher.